Successful Environmental Management

in a week

Mark Yoxon

Headway · Hodder & Stoughton

Cataloguing in Publication Data is available from the British Library

Yoxon, Mark
    Successful environmental management in a week
    1. Environmental engineering   2. Environmental protection
    3. Buildings – Environmental engineering
    I. Title   II. Institute of Management
    658.4'08

ISBN 0 340 66374 X

First published 1996
Impression number   10 9 8 7 6 5 4 3 2 1
Year   1999   1998 1997 1996

Typeset by Multiplex Techniques Ltd, St Mary Cray, Kent.
Printed in Great Britain for Hodder & Stoughton Educational,
a division of Hodder Headline Plc, 338 Euston Road, London
NW1 3BH by Redwood Books, Trowbridge, Wiltshire.

the Institute
of Management

F O U N D A T I O N

The Institute of Management (IM) is at the forefront of management development and best management practice. The Institute embraces all levels of management from students to chief executives. It provides a unique portfolio of services for all managers, enabling them to develop skills and achieve management excellence.

For information on the benefits of membership, please contact:

Department HS
Institute of Management
Cottingham Road
Corby
Northants NN17 1TT
Tel: 01536 204222
Fax: 01536 201651

This series is commissioned by the Institute of Management Foundation.

C O N T E N T S

Effective environmental management makes business sense. Good businesses are already serious about environmental management and are responding to the new green commercial pressures in ways which ensure they and their constituents have a future. These pressures – working through legislation, technical and market developments, and the consumer – are here to stay. Organisations must integrate environmental considerations into business activity – and be *seen* to be doing so.

These new pressures also bring with them new business opportunities. This practical book has been written for managers who want to cut through the green rhetoric and get to the heart of practical environmental management action that will make sense for their business. The book will help you map out your own route to success:

Sunday	–	What is it all about?
Monday	–	Taking stock
Tuesday	–	Making sense
Wednesday	–	Making it your policy
Thursday	–	Communication and reporting and information systems
Friday	–	Training for success
Saturday	–	Putting environmental management to work

As with any journey, preparation and the right tools and equipment will help you to get where you want to. Environmental management is no different, and by the end of the week you'll be well on your way to success.

What is it all about?

The environmental debate is over. Being green is no longer
fashionable or glamorous, it is a new fact of business life.
Just as the debate about quality and health and safety
several years ago established these factors as cornerstones
of effective business practice, so environmental issues are
here to stay. Speculative questions like 'Will the
environment affect my business?' are missing the key point:
it's a question not of 'Will?', but 'How much?' and 'How
soon?'.

The real questions for business, given this new fact, are
concerned with whats, hows and whens:

- What do I need to do?
- How can I do it?
- When should I take action? (And if I don't, what then?)

Finding the best business answers to these questions is the
raison d'être for this book. The text and exercises included
will help you find your own business-focused answers and
actions.

Before getting into the detail, it is useful to overview the
big picture:

- Why bother with environmental management?
- What are the driving factors?
- What are the business benefits?
- The seven steps to success

Why bother with environmental management?

There are three ways to respond to the environmental issue:

1 Ignore the issue completely and hope that it will go away and not have any business impact at all.
2 Defend your current position, even if it won't stand up to close scrutiny, and keep your fingers crossed that the business won't be affected.
3 Become proactive and do something positive about greening your business in ways which make business sense and save you money.

So why bother with environmental management? The short answer is that if you don't, sooner or later someone else will. This will then *force* you to react and you will lose some control and probably some business along the way –

perhaps through machine downtime, staff diverted from key functions, and management time spent putting things right. Even worse, your business credibility may be damaged. Be wise before problems arise: it's much more effective than fire-fighting *afterwards*. The positive alternative is to adopt a proactive approach and put you and your business *in* control.

What are the driving factors?

Successful businesses respond positively to change and manage that change so as to create new business opportunities. The environment is a force for change which can be separated into six driving factors:

1 the law
2 the fiscal factor
3 consumers and customers
4 staff
5 the community
6 good management.

The law
A growing amount of new and demanding environmental legislation has been brought into force, and all of it affects businesses. From the UK government has come the Environmental Protection Act of 1990 and the Water Resources Act of 1991, and a new wave of legislation has come from Europe – over 400 pieces at the last count covering liability for packaging, waste, discharges and the eco-labelling of products.

Regulators with sharper teeth have been created to police the new legislation. In the form of Her Majesty's Inspectorate of Pollution (HMIP) and the National Rivers Authority (NRA), together with various waste-regulation authorities, these bodies are promised to become the new UK Environment Agency. Local authorities, furthermore, have growing powers to enforce environmental legislation and to act against those industrial processes that most pollute the environment. Through poor management and neglect of this new legislation, it is possible for businesses to lose their licences to operate. Ignorance is not a valid defence.

The fiscal factor
Environmental considerations are increasingly being taken into account in the lending process and are becoming a standard part of loan screening. A requirement to show evidence of effective environmental management systems – both on paper and in practice – is now as important as sound cash-flow management.

In a similar way, satisfying environmental criteria is increasingly becoming a part of assessments by insurance companies. The successful management of environmental issues in your business is a growing requirement on the part of insurers: they may well expect you to carry out a compliance audit of legislation as mandatory before they will provide cover. Second-rate environmental performance will increase your insurance premiums or at worst could result in refusal from insurers.

Customers and consumers

If they aren't doing so already, your customers in the high street, or other companies you supply, *will* be expecting increasingly high-quality products. Environmental criteria are simply another aspect of this growing quality expectation. As supply chains become greener, you will have to manage the greening of your business in order to maintain your position. Already, professional institutions such as the Chartered Institute of Purchasing and Supply have recognised this and are issuing guidance to their members on how to integrate environmental factors into purchasing and supply management decisions.

Staff

Your staff, particularly the highly skilled, are increasingly sensitive to the quality of the environment they work in and the impacts your business may make through its products and sales. The nature of business is changing. With fewer core employees, the real cost of staff absence will increase. Positive steps towards a holistic approach to employee health and satisfaction will reduce staff absence and staff turnover and improve morale. These are measurable benefits to the organisation.

The community

There is increasing recognition that treating the environment as a free resource with scant regard for the future is no longer acceptable. People care about the environment – they use it for sport, amenity and enjoyment – and this is increasingly reflected in their behaviour as consumers, shareholders, employees and citizens. Business is a part of the society it serves and society is becoming increasingly intolerant of the lack of environmental performance. Effective environmental performance will therefore become a *licence to operate*.

Good management

The successful management of your business should yield bottom-line benefits. If not, then you are dead in the water. Successful environmental management is no different. Simple measures such as reducing energy consumption, improving transport operations, minimising waste, changing office practices and even investigating whether your waste can be someone else's raw material will bring environmental benefits. What is more important, such measures will also reduce overheads and save you money.

'The environment', as already mentioned may also represent new markets for your business. DTI estimates suggest that the global market for environmental products and services will be worth in excess of £130 billion.

What are the business benefits?

Perhaps this is the *seventh* driving factor, and very much about 'What's in it for you?'. By assessing the business benefits resulting from effective environmental management, you can begin to balance the investment–return equation. Use the following benefits as a checklist. Although you are not quantifying the returns here, you should begin to get a feel of how you can make bottom-line savings.

	✓ tick
Cut energy costs	☐
Cut waste and disposal costs	☐
Cut transport and distribution costs	☐
Cut water use and costs	☐
Reduce emissions and discharges	☐
Ensure compliance with legislation	☐
Reduce the risk of accidents	☐
Improve staff morale	☐
Easier recruitment and retention of staff	☐
Better community relations	☐
Sustain and develop present markets	☐
Create new customers and markets	☐
Better access to finance and insurance	☐

The seven steps to success

As with all good management, you can't do it all at once. Environmental management is very much like going on a journey, and you need to plan and read the signs along the way to make sure you end up where you want to be. The actual route will vary from business to business, and some of the steps may well be taken alongside each other. As long as you fit them all in along the way, then the journey will be successful. Remember, environmental management is a *process* not a programme, and a process which is *ongoing*.

Step 1 – Taking stock

This is the critical first step on the road to effective environmental management. A systematic review of your past and current environmental position and performance, and the data it reveals, will become your baseline to measure against. It will identify business strengths and weaknesses as well as any risks or threats. Most importantly, taking stock will identify opportunities to combine environmental factors with sound business practice.

Step 2 – Making sense

Once you have taken stock, the next step is to find out what the information gained means in the context of your business, plus the implications of your past, present and future environmental decisions. Making business sense of this data will enable you to make decisions with confidence.

Step 3 – Making it your policy

The perfect environmental policy will be dynamic, flexible, proactive and efficient. By now, you will know where you want to be. The policy formalises your good intentions by nailing your colours to the mast with pride and confidence.

Step 4 – Communication

Managing the environmental communication process will ensure that everyone has both the same map to work from and the tools they need to make environmental management a success.

Step 5 – Reporting and information systems
The way you present your findings and recommendations
will influence how they are actioned. Your strategy will
need to be flexible, acknowledging each of the four
ingredients of a business: people, systems, technology and
site. Your report and the work that underpinned it needs to
become a milestone and not a millstone! To ensure this
happens, you will need to establish functional information
systems which help staff to implement the
recommendations of your report.

Step 6 – Training for success
Without staff commitment – from shop floor to senior
management – all your hard work is going nowhere.
Involving all staff in implementing environmental
management is vital, and can be achieved through effective
training. Senior management must be seen to commit
themselves totally, or environmental management will fail.

Step 7 – Putting environmental management to work
The first six steps are all *investments*. To ensure that they
show a return for the business, you will need to take action:
implement recommendations, change procedures, make
cost savings and involve staff. You need to be SMART!

S pecific	– What will you do?	
M easurable	– How will you know you've done it?	
A chievable	– Can it be done?	
R ealistic	– Can you do it?	
T ime-related	– When will you do it?	

Summary

We have begun the week with a general overview of the
whats, hows and whens of successful environmental
management:

- Why bother with environmental management?
- What are the driving factors?

  - the law
  - the fiscal factor
  - consumers and customers
  - staff
  - the community

- What are the business benefits?
- The seven steps to success:

  1 Taking stock
  2 Making sense
  3 Making it your policy
  4 Communication
  5 Reporting and information systems
  6 Training for success
  7 Putting environmental management to work

Your environmental position – a diagnostic self-check

Before moving onto tomorrow's detailed stocktaking of your
business, now is the time to carry out a quick diagnostic
check of your *current* environmental performance. The chart
opposite deals with some of the issues involved: what areas
might *you* need to consider? The higher your score, the
more rigorous is your management of the issue. Your aim

might be to move your organisation up through the grades towards the best-practice level.

Score	Energy	Water	Raw materials	Process and product	Etcetera ...
4					
3	●				
2		●	●		●
1				●	

How to use the chart

1 Look at each column in turn. Put a mark in the cell which best represents your current position.
2 Once you have completed all the columns, join your marks to produce a graph line. This may be uneven: the peaks will show where your current effort is most refined, the troughs where you may need to do some work. Some issues may be more important than others for your particular organisation.

By working through this exercise, you can begin to focus on environmental issues relevant to your organisation.

The pressures on organisations to demonstrate a commitment to the highest standards of environmental performance, for their staff, their customers, their insurers, their bankers and all their stakeholders, will not go away. The rest of the week considers how to make environmental management work for your business – namely, by following the seven steps in ways which make best sense for *you*.

Your environmental impact – a self-check

Score	Energy	Water	Raw materials	Process and product
4	Formal policy, procedures and action in place to minimise energy use. Purchases considered for energy impacts.	Formal policy and procedures and action in place to minimise water use.	Full environmental analysis, including impact assessment for all raw materials used.	'Life cycle' * assessment of all products from the design stage onwards. Full analysis of all equipment and process impacts.
3	Some procedures in place and actioned in part. Staff encouraged to turn off lights etc.	Some procedures in place, and some activity. The cost of water is monitored.	Some environmental analysis of some materials.	Some information is available, and environmental issues sometimes considered in decision making.
2	Unadopted energy policy set and followed in some areas of the organisation.	No formal procedures, but the conservation of water is considered. Staff encouraged to turn taps off etc.	Environmental option chosen on cost grounds alone.	Limited environmental information obtained or recorded.
1	An unwritten set of guidelines. Little activity or staff involvement on an organisation-wide basis.	An unwritten set of guidelines. Little activity or staff involvement.	Little or no activity to investigate the environmental impacts of chosen raw materials.	Outside health and safety considerations, little else is done to consider impacts.

* See Tuesday

Your environmental impact – a self-check (cont'd)

Site	Paper and packaging	Waste and Discharges	Transport	Suppliers
Buildings maintained to a high standard. Good site conditions always evident. Environmental policy for these issues.	Systems in place to reduce packaging and paper use. Good communication with customers to minimise packaging	Full records. Duty of Care followed. Targets set for waste reduction and recycling.	Organisational transport policy in place which includes environmental considerations	Full environmental analysis of suppliers' goods and services, and excellent communications with them.
Procedures in place for premises and site. Manager tours the site at least monthly.	Some recycling and reuse of materials. Any legal requirements are met.	Good records. Legal requirements met. Waste stream identified. Environmental impact of goods considered.	People and goods journeys planned for maximum efficiency. Driver training as appropriate.	Suppliers are aware you have a policy, and some efforts are made by you to adhere to it in your choice of suppliers
Manager irregularly tours the site. Problems sorted out only as they arise. No policy on premises, site and environment.	Patchy activity, often driven by unit initiatives. No communication with suppliers or customers.	Patchy record keeping. Some reduction and recycling.	Vehicles maintained and serviced to required standards. Public transport used when possible.	Some departments impose environmental criteria on their choice of suppliers.
No monitoring programme or policy. Sometimes, individuals take initiatives.	Activity at an individual-initiative level only or not at all.	Limited records, and no policy or action.	Activity driven by individual initiative only.	Little or no consideration of the environment in your choice of suppliers of goods and services.

Step 1 – Taking stock

Unless you had a perfect score on the self-check yesterday
and can therefore put your feet up and relax, it's time to
roll your sleeves up and start with Step 1 – Taking stock.
As we noted on Sunday, this is the decisive first step on the
road to effective environmental management, and it
involves a systematic review of your past and current
position and performance. *If you want to manage it, then you
need first to measure it.*

Today we're going to look at:

- What is an environmental review?
- Preparing and setting the scope of your review
- Issues and information gathering

Later in the week we'll make sense of the data gathered,
and develop the reporting and information systems so that
the work makes business sense.

What is an environmental review?

A review is simply a preliminary stock check against which future progress can be measured. It provides the baseline and a system for effective environmental management. Carrying out an environmental review will enable you to set out with confidence a plan of action, with business-based priorities and targets clearly identified. The review is the CORE of your work, and it should look at:

C oncerns – What is at stake?
O pportunities – What benefits could be achieved?
R egulations – What must we do?
E xamples of good practice – What are others doing?

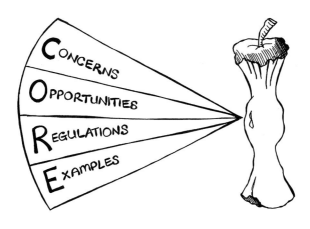

Your goal is to carry out a thorough environmental review of your business – pips and all! Although the detail generated by each part of the review will vary from organisation to organisation, the *issues* remain the same.

By the end of the week, you should be able to answer with confidence any questions raised by the key areas set out earlier.

Preparing and setting the scope of your environmental review

There are five basic questions to answer. By finding your answers to these, you will be able to set the scope of your environmental review, and this in turn will help you to identify both current practices and any learning acquired from past experiences:

1 Why do a review?
2 What can I expect from a review?
3 Where should I focus my efforts?
4 Why do I need to get others involved in the review?
5 How should I plan the review?

Why do a review?
Sunday's chapter of the book should have convinced you of the legal and efficiency arguments for carrying out an environmental review. Conducting such a review will provide a planned management response to these arguments.

What can I expect from a review?
The direct results of an environmental review should include:

• Compliance – confidence that you are complying with existing, and will be able to embrace future, legislation

- Savings – identifying areas where you can start to save money and so gain that competitive edge
- Impacts – understanding where your greatest environmental impacts occur, and reducing associated risks
- Policy – the information to draft a meaningful organisational policy for environmental management
- Action – the information to set an action plan to bring the review to life

Under the heading, 'Benefits from an environmental review', note four or five key benefits you want to see from your environmental review.

Where should I focus my efforts?
Your environmental review will allow you to focus on those areas of environmental management that need attention and those areas which represent the best opportunities for the business. In the beginning, just walk: as you progress, the pace will quicken.

Why do I need to get others involved in the review?
Carrying out the review on your own, in isolation, is a sure way to make the implementation of its findings hard work later on, and all your efforts may, as a result, come to nothing. Teamwork is therefore the key to success, and your 'team' may be drawn from inside and outside the organisation. You need to decide *how much* and *when* your team members need to be involved in the review process. Whatever you do, make sure:

- that senior management are involved and totally committed
- that you have access to specialist skills if necessary. These may come from within the organisation or through developing relationships with professionals – for example, your local environmental health officer – who regulate your business
- that staff know what you're doing and *why* you're doing it
- that those involved understand, and are able to do, what you want them to do

How should I plan the review?
You need to decide the scale of your environmental review. Is it to cover all organisational functions, from offices to transport? Will you focus on some *priority* areas first? Will you look at a specific site or sites? Will you focus on just one or two areas – a partial review – and then build up the full picture over time?

Some questions you might ask in your early team meetings are:

1 Which areas of the organisation are we going to look at? You might already know that energy use and packaging, for example, are causing concern for your business. If the organisation wants to see some action here, then this could be a good place to start your work.

2 What information do we need, and how best can it be obtained? Deciding what information you need is crucial. For example, you might really need to know how much total energy the business uses, and to be able to break this down into heating, lighting, equipment, production and so on. (Although the utility bills will be a starting point, you and your team will need to work out ways to break down this global measure into its component elements). The best ways of obtaining the data will depend on what it is you need to know. Ask yourself: what resources do we have available from internal expertise and records, and external sources of guidance? You will then begin to establish *what* information already exists, *where* it is and *who* keeps it.

3 What is a realistic time scale in which to carry out our review? It is much more desirable to carry out your environmental review effectively than to fail by setting unrealistic goals and targets. Once you know what you are going to do, begin to discuss with your team the best time frame for each element of the review. The driving factors we discussed on Sunday may help you to set your priorities here.

Energy and office equipment

What	Watt	£/week*	£/year*	Worth a look?
Drinks vending machine	3,000–9,000	10–30	500–1500	✓
Large photocopier	3,000	10	500	✓
Telex machine	3,000	10	500	✓
Small photocopier	1,600	6	300	✓
Large fax machine	1,100	4	200	
Computer	700	2.50	125	✓
Printer	400	1.50	75	✓
Small fax machine	150	0.50	25	
Electric typewriter	150	0.50	25	✓
VDU	140	0.45	22.50	✓
Franking machine	90	0.32	16	
Desk lamp	60	0.22	11	✓
Desktop calculator	15	0.05	2.50	
Totals:		£50.00	£2,500.00	

* Week = 40 hours. Year = 50 weeks. Note: the figures and equipment illustrated above are for guidance only – you may have more than one of each piece of equipment.

4 How will I communicate with key staff and staff in general? You should be in a position to move forward to determine the relevant issues and gather the relevant information for your organisation. Before carrying on, now is the time to hold a briefing meeting with key internal staff and to formalise the communication process with staff in general. Staff commitment and

involvement will help ensure success. Your first briefing meeting might well be part of a general management meeting. Include in it the following issues:

- Why are we carrying out an environmental review?
- What is planned? (Perhaps include your own version of the project-outline chart shown below)
- What benefits will we gain from the work?
- The practicalities of the review

The ideas in the chart below will help you build a project outline for your environmental review.

Issue	Score*	What aspects?	When?	Who do we need to get involved? Internal — External
Energy				
Water				
Raw materials				
Process and product				
Site				
Paper and packaging				
Wastes and discharges				
Transport				
Suppliers				

*From Sunday's self-check

Issues and information gathering

Having set your strategy, it's now time to go out and do the work. It would make sense to design some model report forms and key questions both for you and for those you will interview as you gather data about your organisation's environmental position.

- What *issues* do we want to know about?
- Where is the relevant *information*?
- What should we ask to get that information?

The previous chart might be a good starting point and will help to set priorities for both the issues you want to know about and the information-gathering process.

Think back to earlier review-team meetings. You will have come up with a ranking of the nine environmental issues for your organisation. It is worth thinking again about how each of these issues might impact on your business and how they are related to one another.

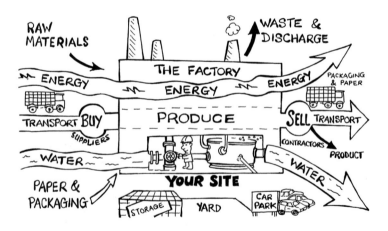

The following provides a quick resumé plus three or four questions, for each of the nine issues, to start you on your information gathering.

Energy

Energy, the fuel that keeps your business running, is a strange and rather abstract concept, a broad and – in many ways – convenient label for various measurable natural phenomena: for example, electricity (measured in *kilowatts*) or the heat found in various items of food (measured in calories).

Organisations can cut an initial 10% off their energy bill without incurring any capital expenditure, a further 10% through investment which rapidly pays for itself, and a further 10% by investing longer term. Saving money and reducing pollution can go hand in hand. Remember: every £1 saved by efficiency measures = a bottom-line saving.

1 How much does your energy cost?
2 Where does it come from – gas, oil, electricity – and where is it used?
3 Where and how could you save on energy costs?

Water

Water is an often-overlooked resource. Turn on the tap and it's there! It is easy to forget, however, that once it comes into the business, you have to *pay* for water, both when you use it for whatever purpose – and when you get rid of it.

1 How much are *you* paying for water?
2 Where are you using or wasting it?
3 Could you change anything to reduce your water use?

Raw materials

The nature of your business will dictate what you buy in as raw material for the production process. Listing raw materials item by item will give you an inventory to work from. You should be able to systematically find out the source of your raw materials and begin to judge the environmental impacts caused along the way. There might be reasonable alternatives that your business could use to reduce these impacts, for example by choosing recycled or reusable materials.

1 What do you buy in, and where does it come from?
2 How efficiently do you use your raw materials?
3 Are there other options which would reduce your environmental impact?

Process and product

The way you operate your processes will impact on the environment. Look again at the simple process model on page 28. Sketch out your own model from the ideas here and add environmental impacts. Similarly, think about your products. Good design can reduce environmental impacts from the start of a product's life to its final disposal.

1 What are your main products, and where is (are) the main environmental impact(s)?
2 How do you operate your production processes so as to minimise environmental impacts and reduce energy and waste produced?
3 Do you train operators in best practices?

Site

Site management offers many opportunities to minimise your exposure to regulation and reduce environmental impacts. Supposing the local environmental health officer turned up tomorrow, would you feel confident about walking him or her around your site?

1 How is your site used, and what do you keep on it?
2 Are the storage methods used appropriate for the materials stored?
3 How well is your site managed?

Paper and packaging

A big issue, this one. The European Union has established a packaging directive setting out specific targets for the recovery and recycling of packaging. Member states have their own targets – the UK has agreed to recover 58% of packaging by 2000. Paper use is a fact of business life. Even the so-called paperless office, promised just a few years ago, has failed to become a reality.

1 Where do you use most paper/packaging?
2 What opportunities exist to reduce materials used?
3 How would your customers/staff respond to any changes?

Waste and discharges

With the new Duty of Care legislation, waste must be managed, and you have a direct responsibility for it. Remember: waste = cost, first when you buy it in as raw materials and again when you dispose of it. Similar legislative requirements apply to the discharges produced as a result of your operations. These too must be managed properly. Have a talk with your regulators and ask for their help and advice – they do want to help business towards best practice.

1 Where are wastes/discharges created in each business activity?
2 Who has responsibility for them?
3 What is the cost to the business in terms of product and disposal?
4 What procedures *are* in place, *could* be in place and *should* be in place?

Transport

A necessity of business life and a significant impact on the environment. Your impacts might arise through your company car fleet, distribution vehicles or use of contract delivery services. Remember, too, that how you *source* your raw materials will have transport implications.

1 How much do you spend on transport – cars, lorries, contractors?
2 How could you reduce transport costs and therefore impacts?
3 Are your vehicles well-maintained and legal, and do you train your drivers?

Suppliers

Even if your own house is in order, it is likely that you will use and be represented by external suppliers and subcontractors. They could potentially undermine your well-laid environmental management plans by not working to your standards.

1 Do your suppliers know what your environmental standards are?
2 Do they know what you expect from them?
3 Do you provide any awareness training for suppliers and subcontractors?

Summary

To devise an effective environmental management system for your organisation, you need environmental knowledge and confidence. Today, by *taking stock*, we have taken the first step on the road to success and begun the planning process for involving others in the work required.

- What is an environmental review?
- Preparing your review:

  - Why do one?
  - What can I expect from a review?
  - Focusing my efforts
  - Who else needs to be involved?
  - How should I plan my review?

- Issues and information gathering:

  - What do we want to know about?
  - Where is the information?
  - How will we get it?

Tomorrow we'll focus on *making sense* of the information you have collected.

Step 2 – Making sense

Yesterday, in Step 1, you took stock of your organisation's environmental position. The issues and information thus gathered now need to make sense for your business. By teasing out the main environmental management issues – both internal and external – you can begin to prioritise your next steps. You should be able to make distinctions between what you *must* do and what you *can* do to improve your environmental management. Before moving forward with your detailed analysis, pause to reflect on what you now know, and:

- Think about your information in terms of people, systems, technology and your site. For each of these, think about:
  - Legislation and standards: do we meet them, exceed them or fall short?
  - Is there an established best practice? What is it? How do we measure up?
  - What do we need to do, what *can* we do and how much might it cost?
  - What procedures might need changing or establishing?
  - How are we performing?

- Draw some brief conclusions from the work, set these out in a straightforward way and take time to talk with colleagues about your findings

This pause for breath is important for you and your colleagues. Involving them again means that you can acknowledge their past help, that they can see what you are making of the data and contribute to the process, and that you are reinforcing the important point that the work is a team effort for the business, not a one person-show.

So now is the time to carry out a more systematic analysis of your findings. There are two areas to work on:

- Are we legal?
- Evaluating the data

Are we legal?

As we noted on Sunday, complying with environmental law is a major obligation for any organisation. This legislation is continuously changing, and the key to success for any organisation is to anticipate any changes and then strive to modify operational practices to stay ahead of them. It is not the intention of this publication to provide a definitive inventory of environmental legislation, and neither is there space to do so. The short section that follows illustrates the main UK and European laws that may need to be considered. The reader is strongly urged to make contact with the regulators noted below to ensure compliance with any legislation relevant to their organisation. Staying legal is the least you need to do. Remember: pollution is now expensive, and even if *you* choose to ignore it, others, with rigorous legislative powers, won't. The UK government has radically overhauled environmental legislation and given the regulators extensive powers to police it. Organisations can be prosecuted in the magistrates' court and High Court, and directors and managers can be held personally responsible for breaches of legislation. Fines of £5,000–£20,000 imposed by the statutory authorities are not uncommon. So it makes good *business sense* to stay legal.

The table on pages 38 and 39 is designed to help you begin to profile the environmental legislation which may apply to your organisation. It is not, however, a substitute for professional advice, which should be sought as a matter of course: your regulators themselves are a good starting point here, and by making contact with them, you will begin to develop a good working relationship for the future.

The European Union is particularly active in the environmental area, with several far-reaching measures in the pipeline, many of which are part of the EU goal of a single market. EC 'legislation' takes three forms:

1 *Regulations* – which are directly binding on the UK and do not require a UK legislative response.

2 *Directives* – which have to be implemented through a UK law.
3 *Decisions* – which, although rare, are binding on the recipient.

Over the next five years, it is expected that 90% of UK environmental laws will have EU origins.

Evaluating the data

Gathering the data was hard work, and will have told you a great deal. The environmental review will have established a baseline which you can use in the future to measure progress against. Evaluating the data is a two-stage process:

- SWOT's going on?
- Making an impact

Some current environmental legislation

Law	Regulator
The Environmental Protection Act 1990 (EPA)	Her Majesty's Inspectorate of Pollution (HMIP)
The Duty of Care – Section 34 of the EPA	Local authority environmental health departments. Waste regulation authorities
Statutory Nuisances – Part II of EPA	Local authority
The Water Resources Act 1991	The National Rivers Authority (NRA) and HMIP in some circumstances
The Water Industry Act 1991	Water companies, the NRA and HMIP
Health & Safety at Work Act 1974 (HSWA). Control of Substances Hazardous to Health 1988 (COSHH). Control of Industrial Major Accident Hazard Regulation 1984, 1988 & 1990 (CIMAH)	Various regulators, including the Health & Safety Executive, depending on the issue
Chemicals (Hazard Information & Packaging) Regulations 1993 (CHIP)	Various regulators
Wildlife & Countryside Act 1981	English Nature, Scottish Natural Heritage, Countryside Council for Wales
Town and Country Planning Act 1990	Any planning authorities

Some current environmental legislation (cont'd)

Notes	Relevant Yes/No
This significant act introduced several new laws and concepts. Part 1 of the Act covers around 5,000 'prescribed processes' covered by 'Integrated Pollution Control'	
The Duty of Care applies to all who import, produce, carry, keep, treat or dispose of waste at any stage in the waste chain. The Duty cannot be delegated to another person. Any breach is a criminal offence.	
The Act contains a consolidated list of items which constitute a statutory nuisance arising as a result of a business activity. Companies are required to bear the costs of clean-up, and personal liability may arise.	
This Act replaced the 1989 Water Act, and deals with discharges to controlled waters – rivers, lakes which discharge into watercourses, ground waters and territorial waters. Under Section 161 of the Act, the NRA can charge polluters for clean-up costs.	
Deals with the control of trade effluent – any effluent from trade premises other than domestic sewage or surface water – to the public sewerage system.	
Examples: HSWA applies to noise in the workplace. COSHH applies to substances hazardous to health CIMAH applies to the storage of specified substances, site management and emergency planning.	
CHIP relates to the classification, labelling and packaging of chemical substances (including wastes).	
Relates to issues around plants (flora) and animals (fauna) which may be influenced by industrial or development activity.	
Relates to proposed development activities which may now require environmental impact assessments.	

SWOT's going on?

As ever, SWOT – Strengths, Weaknesses, Opportunities and
Threats – analysis is a useful tool for the first trawl through
your raw data. Indeed, you might like to carry out an
initial SWOT analysis for all your findings. For an office
environment, it might look like:

STRENGTHS	WEAKNESSES
Good controls on heating and lighting. Layout makes good use of ambient light. Door self-closing so retaining room heat.	Office machines always on – e.g. computers at lunchtimes. Waste bins often full of paper. Staff overriding heating controls and opening windows to cool the office.
OPPORTUNITIES	THREATS
Establish energy-saver purchasing policy for new equipment. Paper could be shredded as packaging. Workplace action groups could be started.	Cost of wasted heating. Health, safety and environmental legislation.

For your second SWOT, analyse each issue area in turn. A
SWOT for transport might look like:

STRENGTHS	WEAKNESSES
All vehicles maintained regularly to the manufacturer's and legal specifications. Drivers trained in safe and efficient driving techniques.	Some old, inefficient vehicles in the fleet. Transport contractors not well briefed. No vehicle policy.
OPPORTUNITIES	THREATS
Improve scheduling and transport planning. Engage transport staff in a monitoring programme. Consider a transport policy.	Breaches of legislation particularly with old – or contract vehicles or both. The investment cost and potential lack of competitiveness.

By SWOTing each issue, you will build up a comprehensive picture of your organisation's environmental position. Remember to involve once again those staff who helped you compile the data in the first place. Staff involvement is essential to the success of an environmental management strategy. It is much more effective to work *with* your colleagues at each stage in your analysis – discussing the merits of, for example, a transport-monitoring programme – than for them to see this proposed somewhat coldly in your final report.

SWOT will provide you with the broad brush strokes of your analysis plus some of the detail. You may decide to pause here for now and deliver an interim report on your findings to date. This can be a useful next step, especially if this work is new to your organisation and part of the process is to sell the benefits internally. If so, skip the next section for now and move on to Wednesday's advice on reporting.

On the other hand, you may decide that a more detailed evaluation is needed immediately. Perhaps some of your data and the initial SWOT analysis have revealed areas where radical change is needed *now*. This may be because you are in danger of breaching legislative requirements, or because an environmental input to a purchasing decision could bring cost savings immediately. You may therefore decide to do the detailed analysis first to develop your own competence and report more formally later. Whatever you decide on the timing or scope, evaluating your environmental impacts is the next stage in your work.

Making an impact

Your review work will already have revealed the
environmental impacts of your business. You should have
quite a comprehensive dossier for each of your business
activities and functions and be able to put these into an
approximate ranking order. For example, if you are a food-
processing operation, then effluent discharges to sewers
may be your greatest environmental impact. If your core
business is transportation, then this is probably where your
greatest environmental effects arise.

- What is a register of environmental effects?
- Know your effects
- Record the information
- Target improvement

What is a register of environmental effects?
At the time of writing, there is no agreed format for
producing a register of environmental effects, though such
a register is a requirement for all new standards such as BS
7750, EMAS and ISO 14001. Whether you want it for one of
these standards or not, it is an excellent way of condensing
your raw data and focusing on priorities for your business.
A register will bring together your work to date in a form
which can be *used* by the business. For it to be effective, it
needs to:

- provide a rigorous 'point of reference' document for
  internal and external use
- be kept up-to-date and accurate
- be usable by colleagues who need to understand and
  act on the information

In short, it needs to make sense of your data in the context of both your business and the six driving factors we looked at on Sunday.

Know your effects

With your raw data to hand from Monday's environmental stock-take, you have already documented the environmental impacts of your business. The technique is now to evaluate each of these nine issues in turn and consider their relative significance. Draw up an evaluation checklist as shown below and score each issue against it. Use a simple scoring system:

- If the issue is unlikely to cause an environmental effect in this area, score it 1
- If the issue may cause an environmental effect, score it 2
- If the issue is very likely to cause an environmental effect unless managed, score it 3
- If the issue will definitely cause an environmental effect unless managed, score it 4
- If the issue is of high concern and therefore an urgent priority as a potential environmental effect, score it 5

Record the information

Using the ideas above, you should be able to produce an environmental-effects sheet or record for each issue area. Of course, many of your issue areas from Monday's work will need to be broken down into their components and run through the evaluation. For example, waste could break down into factory waste, office waste, raw-materials waste, canteen waste and so on. You need to decide how many or how few subdivisions to make for each issue.

An evaluation checklist for environmental impacts

What to consider	Energy	Water	Etcetera...
What do we know? Advice from regulators, industry associations and scientific knowledge may point to an issue in your business with potential to cause an environmental problem or effect. For example, the use/disposal of an organic solvent will have a high ranking.			
Health and safety issues Something you use may have the potential for an in-house or external effect. For example, your paint-spraying process may result in discharges to the atmosphere.			
The law Your operations are likely to be regulated, and fall under several legislative requirements – for example, the Duty of Care.			
Stakeholders The perceptions of stakeholders (see Sunday) about your operations may be of significance. For example, your factory may border a site of natural importance.			
Resources The raw material you use in your processes may raise issues about sustainability or ethics. For example, you may use tropical hardwoods or precious metals.			
The possibility of an effect Some aspects of your operations might cause an environmental effect. For example, if you transport bulk chemicals, then the time when the vehicles are on the road will bring the greatest chance of such an effect.			
Finance and insurance Some aspects of your operations might have more potential to bring a cost penalty. For example, a yard spill or breach of a bund might result in a costly river-pollution incident.			
Compliance with your policy Your developing environmental policy (see Wednesday) may commit you to achieving certain targets. For example you may make a commitment to reducing waste produced by 15% – is this realistic?			
Total score:			

To complete your register, you need to do two more things:

1 add supporting information
2 bring it together as a comprehensive, stand alone and user-friendly document.

Add supporting information
Although the data and analysis on their own will mean a great deal to you and any colleagues closely involved in its compilation, to make it usable by *others* in the organisation it needs some supporting information. Most of this supporting information will already be to hand in one form or another. Now is the time to write it down. For each of the headings below, simply write up the notes – mental or otherwise – that you have made.

1 When the work was done.
2 Who did the work – i.e. either you or colleagues under your direction (or both).
3 The extent of the evaluation – e.g. which issues were covered, and in what detail.
4 Who will follow through any recommendations or necessities.
5 A short resumé for each issue area, noting significant effects and what you propose to do to manage them.
6 A ranking of your environmental effects from major to minor.
7 When the process will be repeated.
8 An appendix with the collected raw data.

Bring it together
If it is to work for your organisation, the register needs to be comprehensive and user friendly. It needs to be accessible to all staff, from those who will need the detailed

information it contains to employees in general to whom it will demonstrate your commitment to environmental management. Bring the whole work together into one well-produced document. Use the headings noted above. Produce multiple copies as reference documents for staff who need the information on a regular basis. Consider adding a straightforward summary of 1–2 pages which might be extracted for general circulation to all staff.

Target improvement
Remember the first exercise from Sunday – the preliminary stock check of where you are now. Your goal was to smooth out the 'graph line', by working to increase your score in each area and so reduce your environmental impact, to stay legal and to look for areas where improvement or changes to your strategy will produce cost savings. This early assessment provided a skeleton upon which to build, and by now you will also have fleshed out the detail. If you stop here, however, the process will grind to a halt or worse still slide backwards. You need to demonstrate to your stakeholders that you are serious about your commitment to environmental management, and most of all, your investment needs to start to show a return for your business.

Think about each issue area again and consider what you need to do. The table overleaf will help summarise your thoughts.

The register, on its own, is an important document for your organisation. Tomorrow and on Saturday we'll look at adding a number of other sections to it, so building it up into a comprehensive environmental management manual for your business.

Area of business	Effect score	Must do – for example, a legal or cost-saving necessity	Will do – for example, an investment in new, more efficient plant	Could do – a longer-term action which could bring benefits
Energy				
Water				
Raw materials				
Process and product				
Site				
Paper and packaging				
Discharges				
Transport				
Suppliers				

Summary

The legwork and interviews you did to gather the information on Monday doubtless revealed much about your environmental position. Today's work, to make sense of it and to evaluate your impacts, will have formalised your initial thoughts in a much more systematic way. You now have the baseline to work from for the rest of the week, and should already be able to deduce what you need to do. By now, you should have:

- made sense of Monday's raw information
- begun to analyse legislation that applies to your organisation
- SWOTed the data by issue or by business function – or both
- analysed, ranked and recorded your key environmental impacts
- set some targets for improving your environmental performance

Tomorrow we'll look at making environmental management your *policy* by bringing together your work so far into a formal *policy statement*.

Step 3 – Making it your policy

By now you will have taken stock, gathered the information about your business and mapped out your environmental effects. All this information, however, is of limited use in isolation. Today we will begin to put it to work for the business by developing an environmental policy.

- Why have an environmental policy?
- What is it?
- Designing a successful policy
- Ingredients for a successful policy
- What to do with your policy

Why have an environmental policy?

It is claimed that 90% of environmental problems are a result of the lack of an environmental policy and the lack of management systems to put it into practice.

A policy should be good for business. If not, it will disintegrate when it faces commercial or economic pressures.

The business benefits of an environmental policy are as follows:

- Your policy is your commitment to the stakeholders in the business – your customers, suppliers and employees. As we saw on Sunday, there are several driving factors for change. All have an interest in and influence upon your business
- Investors and insurers want to know that you are managing your business without environmental damage and without any of the risks associated with poor practice
- Stricter environmental legislation will put pressure on your business either directly, because of your operations, or indirectly because those you supply insist on dealing with green suppliers. By being proactive you can anticipate change, tune your management systems accordingly and keep one step ahead of the competition
- Pressure from your local community and from consumer and campaign groups will grow. Your policy is one positive response to these pressures
- Environmental costs and responsibilities are increasing. Your policy means you are tackling the issues in a direct way
- Businesses that have addressed environmental management have reported increased staff motivation. Recruitment and retention may well be improved by having an active and efficient environmental policy

What is it?

Basically, an environmental policy is a short written statement explaining your business position on the environment. Everything in the statement should fit onto a single side of A4, or perhaps a pocket-sized card. This policy statement – which is similar to a health-and-safety (H&S) or TQM policy statement – has three functions:

1 It identifies the key issues for your business.
2 It says in broad terms what you will do about them.
3 It gives an overview of what you will do to monitor and improve the environmental performance of your business.

An environmental policy differs, on the other hand, from H&S or TQM in that environmental enhancement is a relative rather than an absolute yardstick.

There are no firmly established requirements about what an environmental policy should achieve. As the BSI's Environmental Management Systems Standard (BS 7750), the international ISO 14001 series and the European Commission's new Eco Management and Audit Scheme (EMAS) become more established, the status of an environmental policy will change.

For your policy to work, it must be dynamic, flexible, proactive and ongoing.

Designing a successful policy

If your policy is to work for you, there are five key areas which you should incorporate into your plan – the five straight 'A's.

Policy design – the five straight 'A's

- Attitude
- Accuracy
- Adequate resources
- Awareness
- Action

Attitude

To establish an effective policy, everyone in the business needs a positive environmental attitude. Commitment and responsibility throughout your business is the glue that holds the policy together. Involving line managers in the drafting of your policy and ensuring that they understand both the policy and its implications for the business are essential tasks. Making sure that the final version is signed off by the chief executive is vital.

Accuracy

Your policy must be a milestone not a millstone. You will
need to set out your goals in an open and honest way. The
recipients of the policy, whether customers or staff, will need
to see that what you have set out is realistic for your business.

Adequate resources

Adequate resources will be needed to bring the policy to
life, so that it is not just a paper exercise which wastes
everyone's time. Resources will include staff time and
some investment of money. The mix and allocation will
depend on your priorities.

Awareness

Effective communication, both within the business and
externally, is essential. The actions of your staff will bring
credibility and credit to your organisation. Staff will need to
be able to integrate the policy into their own activities in the
workplace. For you to maximise your new environmental
stance, your customers and suppliers will need to know
what you now expect from them. And on a wider front,
your community – from the local to the national or
international – will need to know about your new position.

Action

Environmental management is a journey and not a
destination, and the policy should reflect this by indicating
how you will monitor, audit and act.

Ingredients for a successful policy

Your policy mix should include a set of specific statements
for your business, including:

- a broad statement of intent. For example:

  Mallonox Ltd is committed to producing and delivering quality products. We recognise that our day-to-day operations impact on the environment in a number of ways. We wish to minimise the potential harmful effects of such actions wherever and whenever this is practicable.

- statements on specific issues emerging from your work on Monday and Tuesday, e.g. energy and raw materials
- a statement of what you expect from third parties, e.g. suppliers and contractors
- a statement indicating that management systems will be developed to implement, review and update your policy

By carrying out the activities specified earlier in the week you've already got most of these statements ready. So start mixing!

The final mix and balance of ingredients will depend on which environmental issues you identified as priorities for your business. An example policy is shown opposite.

IN Form Training & Communication
Environmental Policy Statement

IN Form is committed to produce and deliver quality professional training programmes. The business recognises that its day to day operations impact on the environment in a number of ways. *IN* Form wishes to minimise the potential harmful effects of such actions wherever and whenever this is practicable.

IN Form is committed to achieving environmental best practice throughout its business activities by:

- ensuring our activities are safe for our employees, associates, delegates and others who come into contact with our work
- complying with or exceeding legal requirements
- accepting reasonable responsibility for any harm to the environment caused by our activities and taking reasonable steps to remedy any damage
- monitoring purchasing practices and internal operations including energy and transport to ensure best use of natural resources and minimum environmental impact
- whenever possible reducing the environmental impact of goods and services supplied by adopting a 'cradle to grave' assessment and responsibility for them
- minimising the waste produced in all parts of our business
- monitoring and working with our suppliers and other third parties associated with our business and setting them similar high standards
- seeking to integrate environmental considerations into future business policy decisions
- ensuring associates understand and are accountable to these policy goals through communication and training
- communicating the policy as appropriate to customers and suppliers
- developing systems to implement and review this policy

What to do with your policy

By now you should be in a position to put the policy together. There are several things you need to do with it:

- Mail a copy of the policy statement, together with a suitable letter of commitment from senior management, to the homes of all employees
- Put copies of the policy on noticeboards and in employee handbooks
- Publish the policy in company reports and catalogues
- Ensure staff awareness of the policy by building it into induction and other training programmes
- Go public. For example, let your suppliers and customers have a copy of your policy, and let them know your expectations of them. You may also want to let the local media know what you are up to and why
- Measure the *impact* of the policy to ensure that the message is being received, understood and acted on

... and the most important final step:

- Keep it up to date. It may make sense to review the policy from year to year. Re-issue it to people on an annual basis, and let them know how the business is performing against its policy objectives

Summary

Your environmental policy and a management system to bring it to life should contribute to the overall viability of your company. In this chapter we have:

- looked at why having an environmental policy makes sense
- looked at the components of such a policy
- provided the building blocks to help you design your own business-specific policy
- looked at what to do with it once you have it!

Your environmental policy is one step on the road towards environmental excellence. Tomorrow we'll look in more detail at the communication process and at reporting and information systems – the next steps to implementing your environmental management system.

Step 4 – Communication, and Step 5 – Reporting and information systems

As Sir John Harvey Jones observed, 'It is easier to declare intent than to carry it out'. By now – having taken stock, evaluated the information, begun to report and drafted your first environmental policy – you will have an excellent awareness of what your organisation *is* and *is not* doing, *needs* to do and *could* do. If you stop here and confine your hard work to the filing cabinet, then you are missing the most important ingredient for successful environmental management: bringing your recommendations to life. Over these final days we will begin the process of making environmental management work effectively for you.

When a person communicates with a colleague, they are conveying ideas and feelings – both essential components to effective teamwork, and the key components of the communication process. Communication is not just about telling people things – this suggests it is only a one-way activity, and assumes that the recipient is listening and knows what you are talking about! A group of people must be able to *share* ideas and feelings with one another. Without this sharing they are only able to operate as individuals. So, if your environmental management programme is to work, then the communication process in turn needs to be managed. Communication is indeed essential for successful environmental management.

Many of the ideas that environmental issues bring to the workplace, and the changes in behaviour which will be required, are new ideas. We need to influence staff understanding, attitudes, and behaviour. Everything you do in your organisation communicates something. Dirty and poorly maintained washrooms may say to staff 'We don't really care about your welfare here' and will result in the negative message being carried by staff to the workplace. Your staff will respond to what you are communicating, whether you have communicated it knowingly or not, and the outcome may not be in tune with what you want to achieve. Staff represent the greatest threat to any project *and* the greatest potential aid to its success. Without your employees on your side, the best laid environmental management plans will fail. On the other hand, if staff are sold on the ideas in your environmental management plan, then the project will almost run itself. Every aspect of staff communication must reflect your organisation's commitment to working towards the highest standards of environmental management. Remember, for the whole organisation, environmental management is a journey and not a destination. Making sure everyone has the same map to work from and all the tools they will need are the keys to successful communication and training.

In this chapter we will look at:

- Internal communications
- Implementing a communication system
- Information systems and reporting
- External communications

Internal communications

To communicate effectively, you need to think about where you are now and where you want to get to. If someone is standing on your foot, for example, then effective communication will remove the source of the discomfort quickly. A communication programme for your environmental management strategy is not really very different – it just has more parts to it. Communication can be considered in four categories:

- Informing
- Instructing
- Motivating
- Seeking

Informing

You might simply need to give staff the information required to change their actions. This could, for example, be:

- 'Our waste-disposal costs have risen by 16% this year because we are not segregating our waste properly' (a straight fact)
- 'I think we could save at least 10% of our lighting costs if we switched off lighting when it is not needed' (your interpretation of facts)

Instructing

Instructing is a much more directed communication, usually with a specific purpose in mind. For example:

- 'Now that we have new waste-segregation bins by each machine, I want you all to make sure they are used'
- 'From Monday, office heating thermostat valves will be set by the office manager only and then adjusted as required'

Motivating

Although instructing is fairly cut and dried, if your initial communication didn't work, motivating, persuading or encouraging might then be necessary. Again you are looking for specific changes in behaviour, and here the change will often be more sustained because staff have bought into the merits of the change. Motivational communication might be:

- 'I know we have been sending lorries out half-full, and I'd appreciate your advice on how to achieve a more effective distribution of our products'

- 'My figures show that your department's energy costs have dropped significantly this quarter. I'd like to thank you and your team for this splendid work'

Seeking

Here, instead of telling staff yourself, you are getting *them* to tell *you*. Asking questions, setting tasks, or simply keeping quiet in a briefing meeting and letting others bring forward their ideas will all achieve the desired result. For example:

- 'I think we could shave a good percent off our transport costs by looking at delivery and routing schedules. I'd like you to look at this and report back at next month's meeting'
- 'How much do we spend on packaging? Are there any other options we haven't looked at?'

Your review and policy work will already have revealed actions you need to take and the relative importance of each. You can now begin to map these against your communication tactics so as to build up your plan of action. Use the ideas in the table below to draft your own 'communication needs' plan of action:

Issue	Required outcome	Informing	Instructing	Motivating	Seeking
Waste	Staff to segregate waste using bins provided.		✓	✓	
Transport	Staff to plan more efficient vehicle routings.	✓			✓
Energy	Staff to switch lights off when possible.	✓		✓	
And so on for each issue ...					

Implementing a communication system
Having decided on the desired outcomes to match your priorities, you now need to consider the three 'M's of implementation:

- Mix
- Media
- Methods

Mix
Of course, to be successful in your strategy you will need to combine two or more categories of communication. For example, if you have legal obligations under the Duty of Care, then *formal instructions* to those staff involved is essential, and 'motivating' and 'seeking' will be of secondary importance. How the mix is determined will depend on your required outcomes.

Media
Make sure you choose the right medium for your communications. A letter from the managing director, sent to every member of staff, will probably be the best way of communicating that your new environmental policy, and the actions it implies, is a significant document for the organisation. Using your notice boards and in-house newsletters is also a good way to raise awareness of your communication campaign.

Methods
A series of presentations, appended to existing staff meeting and briefing systems, will probably be the best way of beginning the communication process with functional groups of staff. It might make sense to prepare a short and punchy version of the report for all staff. Adding specific examples to match each audience group will help their identification with the overall strategy.

Information systems and reporting

By now your data will be in a usable form and your
intentions declared in the environmental policy that you
drafted yesterday. However, the information you have
collected and analysed must not stagnate – it needs to *flow*.
We therefore need to look at the following:

- Why establish information systems?
- What to set up?
- Ways to design your system
- Reporting

Why establish information systems?
The work you carried out earlier in the week to assess your
environmental position and the business sense you made of
it need to be effectively integrated with how the business is
managed. Implementing environmental management will
require changes, and you will need to be able to show that
these changes are making sense by quantifying the benefits
to your organisation. Take just one part of your work,
perhaps on waste management. The chart opposite shows
who might need to know about your work.

Waste management information

Who needs to know?	What might they need to know about?
Production manager	Your analysis of volumes of waste being produced and the estimated cost. Recommendations for modifying aspects of the production process so as to reduce waste. The benefits of changing practices – estimated and actual.
Site manager	The impact on site management of introducing skips for waste segregation. Responsibilities for managing any new arrangements, including relationships with waste contractors.
Purchasing manager	Changes in purchasing patterns and the sourcing of materials. Suppliers' attitudes and involvement.
Your regulators, for example your local environmental health officer or waste regulation officer	How you are recording waste-management data under your Duty of Care regulations. The data itself.
External stakeholders such as insurers, financiers, suppliers, contractors and the local community	That you are reducing the production of any hazardous wastes. That you are sourcing new process materials – for example, replacing organic solvents with a detergent based process.

To satisfy such a diverse range of information needs, you must establish a rigorous, dynamic and ongoing information system.

What to set up?
Whatever information system you set up, it needs to be *accessible, accurate* and *adjustable.*

Accessibility
It is worth spending a little time writing down who you think will need access to the information and *why* they might need that access. Begin by drafting out a sheet for each of the nine environmental issues you began with on Monday. Ask yourself three questions, to be applied both internally and externally to your organisation:

1 Who have you already talked to?
2 Who will you need to talk to?
3 Who will want to talk to you?

Finally, add your answers to two more questions:

1 What might they need to know?
2 What do I want them to know?

The example on waste management above should give you some ideas here.

Whatever you come up with from the work above, your information system needs to include:

- legislative requirements
- health-and-safety requirements – including COSHH
- records of existing consents and licences relating to emissions and discharges
- a summary of your 'stock-take' from Monday

Accuracy

Your measurements on Monday and Tuesday will have
begun to quantify your environmental performance and
provide a baseline to measure progress against. Accuracy
is a vital component in substantiating the validity of your
work. Compare the impact of these two statements:

- 'I think we should be reducing our energy costs because
  we'll save money and help the environment'
- 'Last year, our energy costs were £x on gas and £y on
  electricity. I have calculated that by fitting better heating
  controls and PIR switches in toilets and break rooms at a
  cost of £z, we would save 6% on our total energy bill
  and pay back the investment in 10 months'

Accuracy is the key to persuasive argument and action.
Your information system therefore needs to be accurate and
specific.

Adjustability

As we have noted earlier, environmental management is
ever-changing. Legislation changes, technologies and
techniques evolve, people are recruited or move on and
your operations change over time. All these changes, most
of which are outside your control, *will* happen. Your
evolving information system thus needs to take account of
change. The third design prerequisite is therefore to make
sure that your system is adjustable.

Ways to design your system

Your 'information-needs analysis' will have told you, as
Abraham Lincoln might have put it, that:

- some of the people will need some of the information for some of the time,
- most of the people won't need the information for most of the time, and
- some of the people will need all of the information all of the time – probably just you!

Your information system therefore needs to acknowledge the *ways* in which the information will be used.

One way to design your system is to consider two related parts:

1 *The hard statistical data.* Although the actual measurement and monitoring might involve recording on paper, it makes sense to go electronic as a way to ensure the data is quickly on hand in the form or forms in which it is needed. Most computer databases can be modified to suit your needs, and there are a growing number of dedicated software packages appearing on the market. Whatever route you choose, you need to be in control. Make sure the system meets your information-storage needs and can handle your raw data. Remember that some data, relating to regulated processes, needs long-term storage and retrieval.

2 *The paper.* You will want some data, from your stock-take and process measurements, readily accessible in your own files. Some of your information will be needed in an easily retrievable paper form – for example, a waste-transfer note to meet the 'Duty of Care' regulations or your discharge consent from the NRA. Set up an indexed, paper-based system to handle this data, and lodge copies with relevant staff who need access.

For both your computer- and paper-based information, you should make sure that:

- you set up maintenance systems to keep the information up to date. It may make sense to delegate some of the responsibilities to staff concerned more directly with the issue
- you indicate who collected the data, when it was collected and how it was collected
- you set out how the data was analysed plus any actions arising from this analysis
- you note cross-links with, for example your health-and-safety policy and practices
- you note how long the data must be kept
- you note the level of confidentiality of the data and who has access to it and for what purposes

Reporting

If you have really worked hard to get this far, then your colleagues will have an inkling of what you have been up to for these past four days (though it might have taken a little longer!). Some members of staff, however, might not be so knowledgeable and will be wondering just what you have been doing poking around the workplace looking for clues.

It's now time to produce the first report on your work. This draft – and do make sure that everyone knows that that's just what it is – produced with the colleagues involved in the process is an excellent way to test the wisdom of your assumptions, conclusions and recommendations.

To draft a successful report, consider the following:

- Discuss the findings with all involved in the process
- Summarise the findings
- Use diagrams or charts whenever possible
- Having identified 'must do' and 'could do' areas, you now need to be more specific and add actions, timescales, costs and benefits. You could think about and factor in the cost of inaction which might well threaten areas of business operation
- Keep the report simple – but perhaps produce variations to suit different target audiences

And think about the content of your first draft:

- A summary
- The purpose of the work
- The objectives of the work
- Areas examined
- Key findings
- First recommendations
- Suggested targets
- The action plan
- Implementation and review

Your next step is to present and circulate the draft for comment to relevant staff. As at the start of the whole process, make sure your senior managers are involved and totally committed.

External communications
The final part of your strategy is to think about your external communications. Many of the stakeholders we looked at on Sunday will have an interest in your environmental record. The purpose of good public-relations work is to establish and maintain confidence and understanding. Many of the points made earlier today – about types of communication and mix, media and methods – apply here too.

To formulate an external-communications strategy, ask yourself some questions:

Why do we want to tell stakeholders what we are doing?
A good PR campaign based on your environmental management work might bring new business, a local environmental management award, better insurance rates, a profile which means prospective employees will choose your organisation, better community relations, and better understanding between you and your suppliers or customers so that your needs are met.

What do they want to know?
The local environmental health officer will want to know you are serious about your implementation of environmental strategy – especially the legal aspects. An environmental pressure group may want to know about your emissions into the air and water, or about your choices of raw materials.

What do we want them to know about?
Above all else, tell stakeholders about your positive
activities past and present. People don't want to hear about
your intentions, no matter how splendid they may seem on
paper. Your actions must exemplify your words if
stakeholders are to believe you are serious about
environmental management.

How can we communicate with them?
Think carefully about your ways of communication. Whilst
you can control what you write on a press release, once it
has been received by the reporter, their own agenda may
eclipse or reinforce your words. And don't forget your
own staff. If you have implemented a serious internal-
communications and training strategy, then each member
of your staff effectively becomes an ambassador for the
organisation. People believe what their peers/friends tell
them. What would your staff say about your organisation's
environmental position? Other effective ways to
communicate require you to take the initiative by
establishing direct relationships with your constituents –
local schools, local people and your local democratic
systems.

As Georg Winter notes in *Business and the Environment*, and
this is arguably the bottom line in any communications:
'Tell the truth, be clear and keep your actions consistent
with words ... It is better to put money into good work
rather than into good reports on mediocre work'.

Summary

The communication process and the systems needed to manage the information are beginning to fall into place now. We have looked at five key issues:

- Internal communications – Informing, Instructing, Motivating, Seeking
- Implementing a communication system
- Information systems – Why bother? What to set up – accessibility, accuracy and adjustability, How to do it – paper work and hard data
- Reporting – Draft, Content
- External communications –Who needs to know what? How to communicate with these people

We'll deal with the training aspects in more detail tomorrow, and return to finalising the report when we wind up on Saturday.

Step 6 – Training for success

The cornerstone of your communication and training strategy is of course training itself. Your goal is to make environmental management work for the organisation, and for the interrelated training to be a success. The following must now be considered:

- What is training?
- Staff engagement
- Establishing environmental training needs
- Training objectives
- Motivating staff

What is training?

Before looking at the detail of training, it is worth spending a little time looking at the principles.

Training: A planned process to modify attitude, knowledge or skill behaviour through a learning experience to achieve effective performance in any activity or range of activities. Its purpose, in the work situation, is to develop the abilities of the individual and to satisfy the current and future manpower needs of the organisation.

Manpower Services Commission, Glossary of Training Terms

Or to put it more simply, training is: 'Any activity designed to improve another individual's performance in a specific area' (Malcolm Peel, *Successful Training in a Week*, also available in this series).

Training and communication are the means by which your organised environmental management activity is unified and the results fed back. Every organisation, from a small business to a multinational enterprise, requires an efficient training and communication process in order to survive and flourish.

Training, and the communication that underpins it, is about skills transfer, motivation, changing attitudes, developing understanding – and the bottom line – action. People will only give their best if they fully understand what the decisions are that affect them, how and why these decisions arose, and how their personal contribution will make a difference. Developing in all staff a sound understanding of *role* is a vital component of the implementation of environmental management.

Training failures and associated communication failures will lead to costly errors and breaches of environmental regulations. Failure can be measured in terms not only of hours lost or fines, but also of the damage to the state of cooperation between the organisation and its clients, customers and – internally – its staff and managers. Either way the outcome is lower morale, and inevitably this will cause damage to the organisation.

Staff engagement

The organisation is a living organism, and as such there is always scope for improvement. In any organisation, the basic strategies for environmental control might be:

1 prevent the creation of any environmental problem in the first place
2 reduce the amount of the problem
3 prevent or control the release of the hazard

4 separate the people you want to protect from the hazard
5 modify the nature of the hazard
6 modify the nature/action of the individual.

Whilst the first five might all be considered procedural mechanisms to control any environmental risk, and only the latter a behavioural strategy, the action of the individual is nonetheless paramount in successful environmental management. Without staff engagement – from shop floor to senior management – then the detailed analysis of the organisation's environmental position, and the work that goes alongside this, such as setting a policy, will not result in positive action. Involving all staff in implementing environmental management is vital.

As we noted on Sunday, the environment brings in driving factors for change from several directions. For an organisation to remain effective, these factors will require responses which bring success to your staff, your organisation(s) – and as a consequence – the environment and the economy.

Training is the key to achieve these successes, and so is inherently of value.

Establishing environmental training needs

It is not enough just to recognise the benefits of training. Successful training must always *change* how people behave and so begin the process of realising the strategies set out in 1–5 on pages 76–7. For these strategies to work effectively, the training solutions necessary must be clearly established.

There are three areas to consider for environmental management training. These can be illustrated as shown in the table opposite.

Strategic training needs
The most important first step in any analysis of training needs is to create a 'big picture' for the organisational needs. This analysis of strategic needs is much more effective than the reductionist analysis which first works out the individual needs and then forms an overall training plan by aggregating the parts.

The starting point for the strategic analysis of training needs should be the business plan for the organisation. Although human-resource implications relating to environmental management might not be explicit in the business plan, they *will* exist. For example, the introduction of a new production process will need staff with new skills to manage and operate the process and manage the environmental implications of the new systems. The new process may produce less waste, but the waste may still need to be dealt with by new on-site storage facilities and a specialist contractor. For the organisation, we can choose to recruit new staff with the skills required or retrain existing

The three areas of environmental management training

Area	What is needed?	Where is the evidence?
Strategic	An examination of the overall picture for the organisation. Long- and short-term organisational needs.	The organisation's business plan. Discussions with senior management (Steps 1 & 2 (Monday and Tuesday) of the environmental review). Your recommendations in Steps 2 and 3 (Tuesday and Wednesday) of the review work.
Functional	An examination and identification of functional training needs.	Your notes and report from the information-gathering stages of the environmental review. Supplementary interviews with managers, staff and customers in identified functional areas.
Individual	The identification of individual training needs to deliver your environmental strategy.	In your environmental review work. Will also require a more detailed analysis which may use existing human-resource and management systems.

staff – or a combination of both. Everyone involved needs to be trained to ensure the best return on investment in new machinery, and to ensure that any negative aspects of *not* training do not become a reality.

A rigorous examination of the business plan, coupled with the knowledge gained in your environmental review work, will begin to reveal the training needs for your organisation. As you address the issues involved, it is worth keeping some questions in mind:

- What are the environmental implications of the organisation's business plan? What are we doing well? Where might we be exposed now and in the future?
- Are staff cognisant of the environmental implications of their work? Are new skills required? How will they be obtained?
- Is the organisation working well enough with respect to environmental requirements? If not, where and why?
- Does the business plan indicate future changes which will have environmental implications and require training interventions?
- Does the business plan infer a culture shift which will require training interventions?

Functional training needs
By looking at strategic environmental training needs, we have established the big picture first. This is the platform upon which the business operates. The second stage in analysing environmental training needs is to identify *functional* and *departmental* issues. Your environmental review work will have revealed training issues in each 'area of business'. You will now need to extend this knowledge using supplementary interviews with managers, staff and customers in identified functional areas.

What is needed to identify functional training needs is some form of environmental *training needs analysis* (TNA). This term encompasses a variety of techniques ranging from the informal and often subjective to rigorous analytical interview techniques designed to detect detailed information. Some questions to keep in mind when examining functional environmental training needs include:

- Which functions and departments represent the greatest environmental strengths?
- Which functions and departments represent the greatest environmental risks?
- What training do we provide already? Is it sufficient to meet functional needs? And if not why not?
- Are the staffing levels sufficient for the job? Is turnover high? What are the training implications?
- What changes are proposed in operational practices? What works well and can be further improved? What will these changes mean for both the operators and for our environmental management goals?
- Where are the gaps in our skills and knowledge?
- How can we measure training effectiveness?

Individual training needs
This step is the final component of your TNA. Whilst the first two steps were concerned with the core and planned business functions, this step engages the activities of the individuals and their individual aspirations. Staff need to be aware of the environmental issues that the organisation is addressing, and of how their actions can influence the environmental performance of the whole business.

Within the organisation, a number of procedures will already exist which directly or indirectly reveal training needs. These include:

- Appraisals/performance reviews
- Tests and examinations – for example, arising out of competence-based training such as Vocational Qualifications
- Self-tests
- Assessments of prior learning
- Mentoring
- Individual career planning
- Career counselling

You could easily introduce environmental aspects into each of these procedures.

Training objectives

Training is not about providing information. It is about the effective management of change, and it involves a combination of skills development, knowledge transfer, the development and support of understanding amongst staff, and – most importantly – sustained attitude change.

Before embarking on a training programme – be it for an individual, an operating unit or a whole department – you will need to consider both the present position of your learners and where you want them to be at the 'end' of the training intervention. Think carefully about any barriers to change, what is realistically achievable in the time frame you have set (or that has been imposed upon you) – and what resources are available for the journey from one side – or several sides – to the other ...

Your training objectives will need to reflect:

- the knowledge that will be needed to underpin your training programme: knowledge about environmental legislation, the organisation's position, demands on employees, demands of customers etc.
- the skills that staff will need to effect change. Some skills will already reside in the organisation but others will need to be introduced through training
- the attitudes staff need to develop in order for them to be active participants in the change process

Good learning takes place when adrenalin flows: passive 'training' activities – for example, watching a video and then being asked to talk about the relevant issues – are a poor substitute for a *dynamic* training process that engages participants in an active way.

Motivating staff

Changes can only be effectively introduced with the accord of the organisation's management team. Any members of the team who are not yet convinced of the need to implement an environmental strategy will *need* to be thoroughly convinced lest they undermine the realisation of that strategy. In most organisations, this commitment to change has to be sanctioned by the directors too.

There are seven areas you need to reflect on before starting a training and communication programme:

1 Considering your own motives and integrity:

- Do I have the respect and understanding of my colleagues?
- Do I practise what I preach?

2 Understanding the person(s) you are going to be working with:

- Can I justify our environmental work in terms which my colleagues in other organisational functions will understand?
- Can I justify and demonstrate our proposed environmental management strategy in ways which ensure respect from colleagues?

3 Underpinning decisions rigorously:

- Am I planning environmental measures well and in time?
- Am I matching my strategy with existing in-house mechanisms?

4 Setting priorities:

- Have I got a medium- and longer-term strategy for the sequencing of environmental implementation?
- Is my strategy realistic, given my understanding of the organisation and the people in it?

5 Finding out what we have to do – legal requirements:

- Set out a schedule of 'must do' requirements aimed at implementing environmental legislation in the organisation
- Ensure that all senior management are aware that environmental legislation *itself* is not debatable – only *the manner of its implementation* is

6 Finding out what will benefit the organisation:

- Set out an inventory of environmental measures that will benefit the organisation
- Report on any success stories once you have hard data to back these up

7 Finding out what else could be done:

- Neutral measures (at zero cost to the organisation)
- Think carefully about whether the organisation has the will or the means to invest in environmental mangement, and the implications of not doing so

Summary

To succeed, you must have the people on your side – not just your staff and 'top team' (who are, of course, the core of your business) but also your customers, your suppliers and the wider community your business operates in. Your training and communication strategy will ensure that your environmental management system comes to life by engaging the people who matter.

Today we have explored:

- what training is and what it can do
- how to engage people – from shop floor to senior management
- establishing your needs – strategic, functional and individual
- your objectives for training – knowledge, skills and attitudes you want to realise
- motivating staff – seven areas to reflect on

Tomorrow is the final chapter and the concluding step on your journey towards successful environmental management.

Step 7 – Putting environmental management to work

By now you will have invested a great deal of time and energy – yours and other people's – into finding the pieces for your successful environmental management jigsaw. Now is the time to fit the pieces together in a way that makes sense for you. On this final day we will look at *implementing* environmental management in your organisation:

- Taking action
- Monitoring progress
- An environmental management manual
- What next?

Taking action

Despite the past six days being characterised by action –
you now need to make things *happen*. Your action plan for
implementing environmental management will draw
together your key conclusions and set out exactly what
positive steps will be taken to realise the benefits for your
organisation. There are three areas to think about in your
action plan:

- What to do
- Targets and goals
- How to do it

What to do
Look again at:

- the data itself from Monday's stock taking:

  - hard facts, for example about energy or raw-materials
    consumption
  - the notes you made, including discussions and
    observations from colleagues with specialist skills

- your conclusions from Tuesday's work to make sense of
  the data you collected:

  - your evaluation of environmental legislation
  - the SWOT analyses
  - your analysis and ranking of environmental impacts

Targets and goals
It might be useful to group your 'to do' list into three
priority areas for action:

- Priority 1: *must do* – those actions which need to be taken, for example to stay legal or bring immediate bottom line savings
- Priority 2: *will do* – those actions which make business sense but are not so urgent, for example those bringing medium-term savings
- Priority 3: *could do* – those actions which may require longer-term planning and investment

Alongside this prioritising of your 'to do' list, you need to add a realistic timetable to start, carry out and finish each action. Whilst it might be desirable to reduce energy consumption by 25% and so save £x on your energy bills, trying to do it all at once is a recipe for failure. As well as any equipment, process or systems changes, positive actions on the part of your staff are the foundation of sustained changes. It is much more realistic to break down your implementation into a series of smaller steps.

An outline action plan

Issue	Goal	When	Players
Energy	Reduce consumption: – heating by 10% – machines by 6% – electricity by 8%	 – March 199? – autumn 199? – February 199?	staff/site manager production manager staff
Transport	Reduce transport costs: – staff cars by 5% – lorry fleet by 10% – contract vehicles by 5%	 – as new vehicles purchased – 1st quarter 199? – 3rd quarter 199?	company-car owners transport manager/ customers contractors
Waste	Reduce waste costs/ increase income: – segregate scrap metals – improve purchasing specifications – reduce office wastes	 – from new skip lease period onwards – at supply contract negotiations – November 199?	site manager/ contractors/buyers/ suppliers waste regulators office staff

... and so on for each issue.

How to do it

Having ranked and set out your environmental action list, you need to give some thought as to how you will carry out each particular action. This is the implementation stage of your action plan, and it has seven phases. The detail for each phase will vary from issue to issue, but as an example:

A transport implementation plan

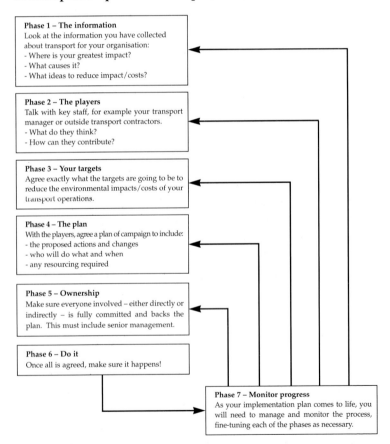

Phase 1 – The information
Look at the information you have collected about transport for your organisation:
- Where is your greatest impact?
- What causes it?
- What ideas to reduce impact/costs?

Phase 2 – The players
Talk with key staff, for example your transport manager or outside transport contractors.
- What do they think?
- How can they contribute?

Phase 3 – Your targets
Agree exactly what the targets are going to be to reduce the environmental impacts/costs of your transport operations.

Phase 4 – The plan
With the players, agree a plan of campaign to include:
- the proposed actions and changes
- who will do what and when
- any resourcing required

Phase 5 – Ownership
Make sure everyone involved – either directly or indirectly – is fully committed and backs the plan. This must include senior management.

Phase 6 – Do it
Once all is agreed, make sure it happens!

Phase 7 – Monitor progress
As your implementation plan comes to life, you will need to manage and monitor the process, fine-tuning each of the phases as necessary.

Monitoring progress

Now that your environmental management system is beginning to slot into place, it is important to verify that what you think should be happening *is* actually happening. For example, in collaboration with one of the regulators, your work might have established a new requirement for emissions from your operations. If pollutants are emitted which exceed the agreed levels, then human health could be jeopardised and penalties could be placed on the organisation. Effective monitoring will avoid such damaging occurrences.

Your progress needs to be monitored on two levels:

• Level 1: the *micro level.* Here you need to monitor progress towards each goal in your action plan and fine-tune the process as your knowledge increases over time. It makes sense to build in a regular monitoring programme as you implement your environmental management action plan. Computer-based information-management systems can be set up to prompt you or your delegates into monitoring progress
• Level 2: the *macro level.* Your stock-take on Monday and your analysis of it on Tuesday have provided the baseline data for the environmental management system you have now put in place. Regular auditing to find out how well you are performing is very important. Even if a business is performing well from a financial perspective, managers still carry out financial audits to verify the results and to prevent any shocks from occurring. Exactly the same reasoning needs to be applied to the verification of your *environmental* performance, which

indeed may be even more important: a breach of
environmental legislation, for example, may have a
devastating effect on the organisation

An environmental management manual

A manual sets out the procedures you have established for
your environmental management system and provides, for
you and your colleagues, the key point of reference for
successful environmental management over the weeks
ahead. It needs to gather users, not dust, and should be
designed for the workplace, not for shelf space!

Now it's time to bring together earlier work into a single
comprehensive and user-friendly document.

*To be effective, your environmental management
manual needs to:*

- be clear and simple
- be written in straightforward not technical language
- be as short and accessible as possible
- use charts and diagrams to bring the information to
  life
- be dynamic and easily updated
- be available to all who need access to it

The manual is really just an extension of the report you drafted on Thursday. By now you should have received comments about your draft. If not, chase your colleagues for their thoughts and ideas.

As with your report following Monday and Tuesday's work, it makes sense to produce a draft manual first and present this to your colleagues.

All that remains to do now is to add an executive summary, present and circulate the draft, and redraft once you have had feedback from colleagues. The manual can then be formally released within your organisation as part of your communication and training processes as developed on Thursday and Friday.

What next?

Way back on Sunday, we noted that successful environmental management is a process not a programme. By now you will have drawn your own map of the territory and gathered the tools you and your colleagues need for the journey. The process should be well in place for your organisation and become simply another component of good management.

For your organisation, this may be enough to provide what you set out to achieve. The implementation of successful environmental management is more than just an obligation or expense: it will provide cost savings and increased profits and market share, and reduce your negative impacts on the environment. Effective environmental management thus also makes business sense.

You should now be able to understand environmental management in the context of your own business. Having travelled this far, you are also in an excellent position to embrace one of the new environmental management system (EMS) standards on page 96.

A checklist for an environmental management manual

Contents	On which day will I find the information?
The purpose of the manual, and a description of your environmental management system.	The culmination of the week's work – in particular Sunday and Saturday – setting out your organisation's needs for a manual and what the manual is.
Your environmental policy	Wednesday.
Issuing specific actions for: – Energy – Water – Raw materials – Process and product – Site – Paper and packaging – Discharges – Transport – Suppliers	Tuesday and Saturday.
Your implementation plans for each issue, including targets and timescales	Saturday.
Roles and responsibilities – the key players	Saturday.
Legislative requirements	Monday and Tuesday.
Communication programme	Thursday.
Training programme	Friday.
Monitoring/auditing programme	Saturday.
Appendices:	
Data for each issue	Monday.
SWOT and environmental effects	Tuesday.
Related policy documents and plans	For example, your health-and-safety policy or supplier policy may be relevant here.
Computer record systems	Notes on what is kept, how it is kept and how to obtain access.
Regulations and permits	Existing records/paperwork.
Notes on any environmental committee meetings	Existing records/paperwork.
Incident reports and emergency plans	Existing records/paperwork.

- British Standard BS 7750: 1994 – Environmental Management Systems
- Eco-Management and Audit Scheme (EMAS) 1993/95 European Standard
- International Organisation for Standardisation (ISO) 14001 – 1996

An organisation with an EMS certified to one of these standards carries a public and clearly recognisable level of achievement, competence and commitment. Such certification will provide *proof* of your efforts.

Enjoy the rest of your journey!

Sources of help and advice

Business in the Environment	Tel: +44 (171) 629 1600
The Environment Council	Tel: +44 (171) 824 8411
Department of the Environment	Tel: +44 (171) 276 3000
Department of Trade & Industry	Environment Helpline: 0800 585794
Energy Efficiency Office	Tel: +44 (171) 276 6200
HMIP & NRA	Set to become the new UK Environment Agency – check with the Dept of the Environment for details
Waste Regulation Officers Environmental Health Officers	Check with your local district or metropolitan council
Green Business Clubs	Check with the DTI

*IN*FORM Training and Communication provides a professional, client-centred range of services which include environmental management training. To discuss your needs, please contact us on tel/fax +44 (1908) 551327.